CALIFORNIA
NATIVE AMERICAN TRIBES

VALLEY
YOKUT TRIBES

by
Mary Null Boulé

Illustrated by
Daniel Liddell

Merryant Publishers, Inc.

Vashon, WA 98070

206-463-3879

Book Number Twenty-three in a series of twenty-eight

This series is dedicated to Virginia Harding, whose editing expertise and friendship brought this project to fruition.

Library of Congress Catalog Card Number: 92-81057

ISBN: 1-877599-45-X

Copyright © 1992, Merryant Publishing

7615 S.W. 257th St., Vashon, WA 98070.

FOREWORD

Native American people of the United States are often living their lives away from major cities and away from what we call the mainstream of life. It is, then, interesting to learn of the important part these remote tribal members play in our everyday lives.

More than 60% of our foods come from the ancient Native American's diet. Farming methods of today also can be traced back to how tribal women grew crops of corn and grain. Many of our present day ideas of democracy have been taken from tribal governments. Even some 1,500 Native American words are found in our English language today.

Fur traders bought furs from tribal hunters for small amounts of money, sold them to Europeans and Asians for a great deal of money, and became rich. Using their money to buy land and to build office buildings, some traders started business corporations which are now the base of our country's economy.

There has never been enough credit given to these early Americans who took such good care of our country when it was still in their care. The time has come to realize tribal contributions to our society today and to give Native Americans not only the credit, but the respect due them.

Mary Boulé

A-frame cradle for girls; tule matting. Tubatulabal tribe.

GENERAL INFORMATION

Creation legends told by today's tribal people speak of how, very long ago, their creator placed them in a territory, where they became caretakers of that land and its animals. None of their ancient legends tells about the first Native Americans coming from another continent.

It is important to respect the different beliefs and theories, to learn from and seek the truth in all of them.

Villagers' tribal history lessons do not agree with the beliefs of anthropologists (scientific historians who study the habits and customs of humans).

Clues found by these scientists lead them to believe that ancient tribespeople came to North America from Asia during the Ice Age period some 20 to 35 thousand years ago. They feel these humans walked over a land strip in the Bering Straits, following animal herds who provided them with food.

Scientists' understanding of ancient people must come from studying clues; for example, tools, utensils, baskets, garbage discoveries, and stories they passed from one generation to the next.

California's Native Americans did not organize into large tribes. Instead they divided into tribelets, sometimes having as many as 250 people. Some tribelets had only one chief for each village.

From 20 to 100 people could be living in one village, which usually had several houses. In most cases, these groups of people were one family and were related to each other. From five to ten people of a family might live in one house. For instance, a mother, a father, two or three children, a grandmother, or aunt or daughter-in-law might live together.

Village members together would own the land important to them for their well-being. Their land might include oak trees with precious acorns, streams and rivers, and plants which were good to eat. Streams and rivers were especially important to a tribe's quality of life. Water drew animals to it; that meant more food for the tribe to eat. Fish were a good source of food, and traveling by boat was often easier than walking long distances. Water was needed in every part of tribal life.

Village and tribelet land was carefully guarded. Each group knew exactly where the boundaries of its land were found. Boundaries were known by landmarks such as mountains or rivers, or they might also be marked by poles planted in the ground. Some boundary lines were marked by rocks, or by objects placed there by tribal members. The size of a territory had to be large enough to supply food to every person living there.

The California tribes spoke many languages. Sometimes villages close together even had a problem understanding one another. This meant that each group had to be sure of the boundaries of other tribes around them when gathering food. It would not be wise to go against the boundaries and the customs of neighbors. The Native Americans found if they respected the boundaries of their neighbors, not so many wars had to be fought. California tribes, in spite of all their differences, were not as warlike as other tribes in our country.

Not only did the California tribes speak different languages, but their members also differed in size. Some tribes were very tall, almost six feet tall. The shortest people came from the Yuki tribe which had territory in what is now Mendocino County. They measured only about 5'2" tall. All Native Americans, regardless of size, had strong, straight black hair and dark brown eyes.

TRADE

Trading between tribes was an important part of life. Inland tribes had large animal hides that coastal tribes wanted. By trading the hides to coastal groups, inland tribes would receive fish and shells, which they in turn wanted. Coastal tribes also wanted minerals and rocks mined in the mountains by inland tribes. Obsidian rock from the northern mountains was especially wanted for arrowheads. There were, as well, several minerals, mined in the inland mountains, which could be made into the colorful body paints needed for religious ceremonies.

Southern tribes particularly wanted steatite from the Gabrielino tribe. Steatite, or soapstone, was a special metal which allowed heat to spread evenly through it. This made it a good choice to be used for cooking pots and flat frying pans. It could be carved into bowls because of its softness and could be decorated by carving designs into it. Steatite came from Catalina Island in the Coastal Gabrielino territory. Gabrielinos found steatite to be a fine trading item to offer for the acorns, deerskins, or obsidian stone they needed.

When people had no items to trade but needed something, they used small strings of shells for money. The small dentalium shells, which came from the far distant Northwest coast, had great value. Strings of dentalia usually served as money in the Northern California tribes, although some dentalia was used in the Central California tribes.

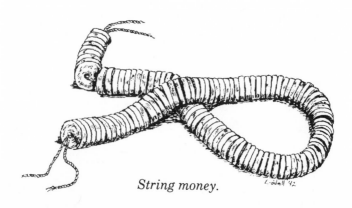

String money.

In southern California clam shells were broken and holes were bored through the center of each piece. Then the pieces were rounded and polished with sandstone and strung into strings for money. These were not thought to be as valuable as dentalia.

Strings of shell money were measured by tattoo marks on the trader's lower arm or hand.

Here is a sample of shell value:

> A house, three strings
> A fishing place, one to three strings
> Land with acorn-bearing oak trees, one to five strings

A great deal of rock and stone was traded among the tribes for making tools. Arrows had to have sharp-edged stone for tips. The best stone for arrow tips was obsidian (volcanic glass) because, when hit properly, it broke off into flakes with very sharp edges. California tribes considered obsidian to be the most valuable rock for trading.

Some tribes had craftsmen who made knives with wooden handles and obsidian blades. Often the handles were decorated with carvings. Such knives were good for trading purposes. Stone mortars and pestles, used by the women for grinding grains into flour, were good trading items.

BASKETS & POTTERY

California tribal women made beautiful baskets. The Pomo and Chumash baskets, what few are left, show us that the women of those tribes might have been some of the finest basketmakers in the world. Baskets were used for gathering and storing food, for carrying babies, and even for hauling water. In emergencies, such as flooding waters, sometimes children, women, and tribal belongings crossed the swollen rivers and streams in huge, woven baskets! Baskets were so tightly woven that not a drop of water could leak from them.

Baskets also made fine cooking pots. Very hot rocks were taken from a fire and tossed around inside baskets with a looped tree branch until food in the basket was cooked.

Most baskets were made to do a certain job, but some baskets were designed for their beauty alone and were excellent for trading. Older women of a tribe would teach young girls how to weave baskets.

Pottery was not used by many California tribes. What little there was seems to have been made by those tribes living near to the Navaho and Mohave tribes of Arizona, and it shows their style. For example, pottery of the California tribes did not have much decoration and was usually a dull red color. Designs were few and always in yellow.

Ohlone hunter wearing deerskin camouflage.

Long thin coils of clay were laid one on top the other. Then the coils were smoothed between a wooden paddle and a small stone to shape the bowl. Pottery from California Native Americans has been described as light weight and brittle (easily broken), probably because of the kind of clay soil found in California.

HUNTING & FISHING

Tribal men spent much of their time making hunting and fishing tools. Bows and arrows were built with great care, to make them shoot as accurately as possible. Carelessly made hunting weapons caused fewer animals to be killed and people then had less food to eat.

Bows made by men of Southern California tribes were made long and narrow. In the northern part of the state bows were a little shorter, thinner, and wider than those of their northern neighbors. Size and thickness of bows depended on the size trees growing in a tribe's territory. The strongest bows were wrapped with sinew, the name given to animal tendons. Sinew is strong and elastic like a rubber band.

Arrows were made in many sizes and shapes, depending on their use. For hunting larger animals, a two-piece arrow was used. The front piece of the arrow shaft was made so that it would remain in the animal, even if the back part was

9

removed or broken off. The arrowhead, or point, was wrapped to the front piece of the shaft. This kind of arrow was also used in wars.

Young boys used a simple wooden arrow with the end sharpened to a point. With this they could hunt small animals like birds and rabbits. The older men of the tribe taught boys how to make their own arrows, how to aim properly, and how to repair broken weapons.

Tribal men spent many hours making and mending fishing nets. The string used in making nets often came from the fibers of plants. These fibers were twisted to make them strong and tough, then knotted into netting. Fences, or weirs, that had one small opening for fish, were built across streams. As the fish swam through the opening they would be caught in netting or harpooned by a waiting fisherman.

Hooks, if used at all, were cut from shells. Mostly hooks could be found when the men fished in large lakes or when catching trout in high mountain areas. Hooks were attached to heavy plant fiber string.

Dip nets, made of netting attached to branches that were bent into a circle, were used to catch fish swimming near shore. Dip nets had long handles so the fishermen could reach deep into the water.

Sometimes a mild poison was placed on the surface of shallow water. This confused the fish and caused them to float to the surface of the water, where they could be scooped up by a waiting fisherman. Not enough poison was used to make humans ill.

Not all fishing was done from the shore. California tribes used two kinds of boats when fishing. Canoes, dug out of one half a log, were useful for river fishing. These were square at each end, round on the bottom, and very heavy. Some of them were well-finished, often even having a carved seat in them.

Today we think of "balsa" as a very lightweight wood, but in Spanish, the word balsa means "raft". That is why Spanish explorers called the Native American canoes, made from tule reeds, "balsa" boats.

Balsa boats were made of bundled tule reeds and were used throughout most of California. They made into safe, light-weight boats for lake and river use. Usually the balsa canoe had a long, tightly tied bundle of tule for the boat bottom and one bundle for each side of the canoe. The front of the canoe was higher than the back. Balsa boats could be steered with a pole or with a paddle, like a raft.

Men did most of the fishing, women were in charge of gathering grasses, seeds, and acorns for food. After the food was collected, it was either eaten right away or made ready for winter storage.

Except for a few southern groups, California tribes had perma-nent villages where they lived most of the year. They also had food-gathering places they returned to each year to collect acorns, salt, fish, and other foods not found near their villages.

FOOD

Many different kinds of plant food grew wild in California in the days before white people arrived. Berries and other plant foods grew in the mountains. Forests offered the local tribes everything from pine nuts to animals.

Native Americans found streams full of fish for much of the year. Inland fresh water lakes had large tule reeds growing along their shores. Tule could be eaten as food when plants were young and tender. More important, however, tule was used in making fabric for clothes and for building boats and houses. Tule was probably the most useful plant the California Native Americans found growing wild in their land.

Like all deserts, the one in southern California had little water or fish, but small animals and cactus plants made good food for the local tribes. They moved from place to place harvesting whatever was ripe. Tribal members always knew when and where to find the best food in their territory.

Acorns were the main source of food for all California tribes. Acorn flour was as important to the California Native Americans as wheat is to us today. Five types of California oak trees produced acorns that could be eaten. Those from black oak and tanbark oak seem to have been the favorite kinds.

Since some acorns tasted better than others, the tastiest ones were collected first. If harvest of the favorite acorn was poor some years, then less tasty acorns had to be eaten all winter long.

So important were acorns to California Indians that most tribes built their entire year around them. Acorn harvest marked the beginning of their calendar year. Winter was counted as so many months after acorn harvest, and summer was counted by the number of months before the next acorn harvest.

Acorn harvest ceremonies usually were the biggest events of the year. Most celebrations took place in mid-October and included dancing, feasts, games of chance, and reunions with relatives. Harvest festivals lasted for many days. They were a time of joy for everyone.

The annual acorn gathering lasted two to three weeks. Young boys climbed the oak trees to shake branches; some men used long poles to knock acorns to the ground. Women loaded the nuts into large cone-shaped burden baskets and carried them to a central place where they were put in the sun to dry.

Once the acorns were dried, the women carried them back to the tribe's permanent villages. There they lined special basket-like storage granaries with strong herbs to keep insects away, then stored the acorns inside. Granaries were placed on stilts to keep animals from getting into them and were kept beside tribal houses.

Preparing acorns for each meal was also the women's job. Shells were peeled by hitting the acorns with a stone hammer on an anvil (flat) stone. Meat from the nut was then laid on a stone mortar. A mortar was usually a large stone with a slight dip on its surface. Sometimes the mortar had a bottomless basket, called a hopper, glued to its top. This kept the acorn meat from sliding off the mortar as it was beaten.

The meat was then pounded with a long stone pestle. Acorn flour was scraped away from the hopper's sides with a soaproot fiber brush during this process.

From there the flour was put into an open-worked basket and sifted. A fine flour came through the bottom of the basket, while the larger pieces were put back in the mortar for more pounding.

The most important process came after the acorn flour was sifted. Acorn flour has a very bitter-tasting tannin in it. This bitter taste was removed by a method called leaching. Many tribes leached the flour by first scooping out a hollow in sand near water. The hollow was lined with leaves to keep the flour from washing away. A great deal of hot water was poured through the flour to wash out (leach) the bitterness. Sometimes the flour was put into a basket for the leaching process, instead of using sand and leaves.

Finally the acorn flour was ready to be cooked. To make mush, heated stones were placed in the basket with the flour. A looped tree branch or two long sticks were used to toss the hot rocks around so the basket would not burn. When the mush had boiled, it could be eaten. If the flour and water mixture was baked in an earthen oven, it became a kind of bread. Early explorers wrote that it was very tasty.

Historians have estimated that one family would eat from 1500 to 2000 pounds of acorn flour a year. One reason California native Americans did not have to plant seeds and raise crops was because there were so many acorns for them to harvest each year.

Whether they ate fish or shellfish or plant food or animal meat, nature supplied more than enough food for the Native Americans who lived in California long ago. Many believed their good fortune in having fine weather and plenty to eat came from being good to their gods.

RELIGION

Tribal members had strong beliefs in the power of spirits or gods around them. Each tribe was different, but all felt the importance of never making a spirit angry with them. For that reason a celebration to thank the spirit-gods for treating them well, took place before each food gathering and before each hunting trip, and after each food harvest.

Usually spiritual powers were thought to belong to birds or animals. Most California tribespeople felt bears were very wicked and should not be eaten. But Coyote seems to have been a kind leader who helped them if they were in trouble, even though he seems to have been a bit naughty at times. Eagle was thought to be very powerful and good to native Americans. In some tribes, Eagle was almost as powerful as Sun.

Tribes placed importance on different gods, according to the tribe's needs. Rain gods were the most important spirits to desert tribes. Weather gods, who might bring less rain or warmer temperatures, were important to northern tribes. A great many groups felt there were gods for each of the winds: North, South, East and West. The four directions were usually included in their ceremonial dances and were used as part of the decorations on baskets, pots, and even tools.

Animals were not only worshipped and believed to be spirit-gods, like Deer or Antelope, but tribal members felt there was a personal animal guardian for each one of them. If a tribal member had a deer as guardian, then that person could never kill a deer or eat deer meat.

California Native Americans believed in life after death. This made them very respectful of death and very fearful of angering a dead person. Once someone died, the name of the dead person could never again be said aloud. Since it was easy to accidentally say a name aloud, the name was usually given to a new baby. Then the dead person would not become angry.

Shamans were thought to be the keepers of religious beliefs and to have the ability to talk directly to spirit-gods. It was the job of a village shaman to cure sick people, and to speak to the gods about the needs of the people. Some tribes had several kinds of shamans in one village. One shaman did curing, one scared off evil spirits, while another took care of hunters.

Not all shamans were nice, so people greatly feared their power. However, if shamans had no luck curing sick people or did not bring good luck in hunting, the people could kill them. Most shamans were men, but in a few tribes, women were doctors.

Most California tribal myths have been lost to history because they were spoken and never written down. The legends were told and retold on winter nights around the home fires. Sadly, these were forgotten after the missionaries brought Christianity to California and moved tribal members into the missions.

A few stories still remain, however. It is thought by historians that northwest California tribes were the only ones not to have a myth on how they were created. They did not feel that the world was made and prepared for human beings. Instead, their few remaining stories usually tell of mountain peaks or rivers in their own territory.

The central California tribes had creation stories of a great flood where there was only water on earth. They tell of how man was made from a bit of mud that a turtle brought up from the bottom of the water.

Many southwest tribes believed there was a time of no sky or water. They told of two clouds appearing which finally became Sky and Earth.

Throughout California, however, all tribes had myths that told of Eagle as the leader, Coyote as chief assistant, and of less powerful spirits like Falcon or Hawk.

Costumes for religious ceremonies often imitated these animals they worshipped or feared. Much time was spent in making the dance costumes as beautiful as possible. Red woodpecker feathers were so brilliant a color they were used to decorate religious headdresses, necklaces, or belts. Deerskin clothing was fringed so shell beads could be attached to each thin strip of leather.

Eagle feathers were felt to be the most sacred of religious objects. Sometimes they were made into whole robes.

Religious feather charm.

Usually, though, the feathers were used just for decorations. All these costumes were valuable to the people of each tribe. The village chief was in charge of taking care of the costumes, and there was terrible punishment for stealing them. Clothing worn everyday was not fancy like costuming for rituals.

Willow bark skirt.

CLOTHING

Central and southern California's fine weather made regular clothes not really very important to the Native Americans. The children and men went naked most of the year, but most women wore a short apron-like skirt. These skirts were usually made in two pieces, front and back aprons, with fringes cut into the bottom edges. Often the skirt was made from the inner bark of trees, shredded and gathered on a cord. Sometimes the skirt was made from tule or grass.

In northern California and in rainy or windy weather elsewhere in the state, animal-skin blankets were worn by both men and women. They were used like a cape and wrapped around the body. Sometimes the cape was put over one shoulder and under the other arm, then tied in front. All kinds of skins were used; deer, otter, wildcat, but sea-otter fur was thought to be the best. If the skin was from a small animal, it was cut into strips and woven together into a fabric. At night the cape became a blanket to keep the person warm.

Because of the rainy weather in northern California, the women wore basket caps all the time. Women of the central and south tribes wore caps only when carrying heavy loads, where the forehead had to be used as support. Then a cap helped keep too much weight from being placed on the forehead.

Most California people went barefoot in their villages. For journeys into rough land, going to war, wood gathering, or in colder weather, the tribesmen in central and northwest California wore a one-piece soft shoe with no extra sole, which went high up on the leg.

Southern California tribespeople, however, wore sandals most of the time, wearing high, soled moccasins only when they traveled long distances or into the mountains. Leggings of skin were worn in snow, and moccasins were sometimes lined with grass for more comfort and warmth.

VILLAGE LIFE

Houses of the California tribes were made of materials found in their area. Usually they were round with domed roofs. Except for a few tribes, a house floor was dug into the earth a few feet. This was wise, for it made the home warmer in winter and cooler in summer. It also meant that less material was needed to make house walls.

Framework for the walls was made from bendable branches tied to support poles. Some frames of the houses were covered with earth and grass. Others were covered with large slabs of redwood or pine bark. Central California

Split-stick clapper, rhythm instrument. Hupa tribe.

villagers made large woven mats of tule reed to cover the tops and sides of houses. In the warmer southern area, brush and smaller pieces of bark were used for house walls.

Most California Native American villages had a building called a sweathouse, where the men could be found when they were not hunting, fishing or traveling. It was a very important place for the men, who used it rather like a clubhouse. They could sweat and then scrape themselves clean with curved ribs of deer. The sweathouse was smaller than a family house. Normally it had a center pole framework with a firepit on the ground next to the pole. When the fire was lit, some smoke was allowed to escape through a hole at the top of the roof; however, most was trapped inside the building. Smoke and heat were the main reasons for having a sweathouse. Both were believed to be a way to purify tribal members' bodies. Sweathouse walls were mainly hard-packed earth. The heat produced was not a steam heat but came from a wood-fed fire.

In the center of most villages was a large house that often had no walls, just a roof held up with poles. It was here that religious dances and rituals were held, or visitors were entertained.

Dances were enjoyed and were performed with great skill. Music, usually only rhythm instruments, accompanied the dances. For some reason California Native Americans did not use drums to create rhythms for their dances. Three different kinds of rattles were used by California tribes.

One type, split-clap sticks, created rhythm for dancing. These were usually a length of cane (a hollow stick) split in half lengthwise for about two-thirds of its length. The part still uncut was tightly wound with cord so it would not split all the way. The stick was held at the tied end in one hand and hit against the palm of the other hand to make its sound.

19

A pebble-filled moth cocoon made rhythm for shaman duties. These could range from calling on spirits to cure illnesses, to performing dances to bring rain. Probably the best sounds to beat rhythm for songs and dances came from bundles of deer hooves tied together on a stick. These rattles have a hollow, warm sound.

The only really "musical" instrument found in California was a flute made of reed that was played by blowing across the edge of one end. Melodies were not played on any of these instruments. Most North American Indians sang their songs rather than playing melodies on music instruments.

Special songs were sung for each event. There were songs for healing sick people, songs for success in hunting, war, or marriage. Women sang acorn-grinding songs and lullabies. Songs were sung in sorrow for the dead and during story-telling times. Group singing, with a leader, was the favorite kind of singing. Most songs were sung by all tribe members, but religious songs had to be sung by a special group. It was important that sacred songs not be changed through the years. If a mistake was made while singing sacred music, the singer could be punished, so only specially trained singers would sing ritual songs.

All songs were very short, some of them only 20 to 30 seconds long. They were made longer by repeating the melodies over and over, or by connecting several songs together. Songs usually told no story, just repeated words or phrases or syllables in patterns.

Song melodies used only one or two notes and harmony was never added. Perhaps that is why mission Indians, at those missions with musician priests, especially loved to sing harmony in the church choirs.

Songs and dances were good methods of passing rich tribal traditions on to the children. It was important to tribal adults that their children understand and love the tribe's heritage.

Children were truly wanted by parents in most tribes and new parents carefully watched their tiny babies day and night, to be sure they stayed warm and dry. Usually a newborn was strapped into a cradle and tied to the mother's back so she could continue to work, yet be near the baby at all times. In some tribes, older children took care of babies of cradle age during the day to give the mother time to do all her work, while grandmothers were often in charge of caring for toddlers.

Children were taught good behavior, traditions, and tribal rules from babyhood, although some tribes were stricter than others. Most of the time parents made their children obey. Young children could be lightly punished, but in many tribes those over six or seven years old were more severely punished if they did not follow the rules.

Just as children do today, Native American youngsters had childhood traditions they followed. For instance, one tribal tradition said that when a baby tooth came out, a child waited until dusk, faced the setting sun and threw the tooth to the west. There is no mention of a generous tooth fairy, however.

Tribal parents were worried that their offspring might not be strong and brave. Some tribes felt one way to make their children stronger was by forcing them to bathe in ice cold water, even in wintertime. Every once in a while, for example, Modoc children were awakened from sleep and taken to a cold lake or stream for a freezing bath.

But if freezing baths at night were hard on young Native Americans, their days were carefree and happy. Children were allowed to play all day, and some tribes felt children did not even have to come to dinner if they didn't want to. In those tribes, children could come to their houses to eat anytime of the day.

The games boys played are not too different from those played today. Swimming, hide and seek among the tule reeds, a form of tetherball with a mud ball tied to a pole, and willow-javelin throwing kept boys busy throughout the day.

Fathers made their sons small bows and arrows, so boys spent much time trying to improve their hunting skills. They practised shooting at frogs or chipmunks. The first animal any boy killed was not touched or eaten by him. Others would carry the kill home to be cooked and eaten by villagers. This tradition taught boys always to share food.

Another hunting tool for boys was a hollowed-out willow branch. This became like a modern day beanshooter, only the Native American boys shot juniper berries instead of beans. Slingshots made good hunting weapons, as well.

Girls and boys shared many games, but girls playing with each other had contests to see who could make a basket the fastest, or they played with dolls made of tule. Together, young boys and girls played a type of ring-around-the-rosie game, climbed mountains, or built mud houses.

As children grew older, the boys followed their fathers and the girls followed their mothers as the adults did their daily work. Children were not trained in the arts of hunting or basketmaking, however, until they became teenagers.

HISTORY

Spanish missionaries, led by Fray Junipero Serra, arrived in California in 1769 to build missions along the coast of California. By 1823, fifty years later, 21 missions had been founded. Almost all of them were very successful, and the Franciscan monks who ran them were proud of how many Native Americans became Christians.

However, all was not as the monks had planned it would be. Native American people had never been around the diseases European white men brought with them. As a result, they had no immunity to such illnesses as measles, small pox, or flu. Too many mission Indians died from white men's diseases.

Historians figure there were 300,000 Native Americans living in California before the missionaries came. The missions show records of 83,000 mission Indians during mission days. By the time the Mexicans took over the missions from the Spanish in 1834, only 20,000 remained alive.

The great California Gold Rush of 1849 was probably another big reason why many of the Native Americans died during that time. White men, staking their claim to tribal lands with gold upon it, thought nothing of killing any California tribesman who tried to keep and protect his territory. Fifty-thousand tribal members died from diseases, bullets, or starvation between the gold Rush Days and 1870. By 1910, only 17,000 California Indians remained.

Although the American government tried to set aside reservations (areas reserved for Native Americans), the land given to the Indians often was not good land. Worse yet, some of the land sacred to tribes, such as burial grounds, was taken over by white people and never given back.

Sadly, mission Indians, when they became Christians, forgot the proud heritage and beliefs they had followed for thousands of years. Many wonderful myths and songs they had passed from one generation to the next, on winter nights so long ago, have been lost forever.

Today some 100,000 people can claim California Native American ancestors, but few pure-blooded tribespeople remain. Our link with the Wanderers, who came from Asia so long ago, has been forever broken.

The bullroarer made a deep, loud sound when whirled above the player's head. Tipai tribe.

Villages were usually built beside a lake, stream, or river. Balsa canoes are on the shore. Tule reeds grow along the edge of the water and are drying on poles on the right side of the picture.

Women preparing food in baskets, sit on tule mats. Tule mats are being tied to the willow pole framework of a house being built by one of the men.

NORTHERN AND SOUTHERN VALLEY YOKUTS

INTRODUCTION

There were three main groups of Yokuts (Yo' koots). The Northern and Southern Valley groups were found in the large San Joaquin (Central) Valley. Their territories covered almost the entire floor of the valley. A third group, the Foothill Yokuts, had territory along the foothills of the Sierra Nevada mountain range, on the east side of the valley.

Altogether, the Yokut tribes owned between 12,000 and 13,000 square miles of land. It is said the Yokuts had more land than any other tribes around them. Historians think the word Yokut meant 'person,' or 'people' in Yokut language.

Population of the pre-history (before white people came) Yokut tribes has been guessed at over 70,000 people. Research shows that the three main groups were made up of about 50 tribelets. Information has been found on at least forty of those tribelets.

California Native American tribes seldom went any farther than fifteen miles from their permanent village in a lifetime. Their tribal languages, as they slowly changed through the thousand or more years, became quite different. As a result, neighboring villages of the same tribe, if they did not visit often, finally could not understand each other.

Therefore, it is interesting to know that the 50 Yokuts tribelets, even though they lived far apart, seemed to have language sounding enough alike that they could be understood from village to village. It would have been like listening to people from Texas today. We can understand what they say but they speak with what we call a Texan accent.

The fifteen tribelets of the Southern Valley Yokuts, some 15,000 people, had territory which went from the lower Kings River, near the modern city of Fresno, south to the Tehachapi (Tuh hatch' a pea) Mountains. Within their territory were three lakes, Buena Vista and Kern Lakes in the south and the much larger Tulare lake further north. Around each of the lakes were huge swamp areas which changed in size every year, depending upon the amount of rain that fell during the rainy winter months.

Thanks to large rivers like the Kern, the Kings, and the Tule, this hot inland valley was kept from being a complete desert; for there were only about five to ten inches of rain a year in this part of the valley. January through March, rain usually flooded the area, filling all three lakes with fresh water. In early summer, melting snow from the Sierra Mountains once again filled the lakes, this time with enough water to keep them from drying up during the long, hot (often-over-100-degrees) summers.

In ancient days the useful tule plants grew canes as tall as twelve feet. In drier areas sagebrush, greasewood, and bunch-grass grew naturally. The only trees were cottonwoods, sycamores, and willow, all of which grew only along river edges. Oak trees, with their important crops of acorn, grew mainly in the low foothills and seldom were found growing very far into the hot valley floor.

Northern Valley tribal boundaries have not been well described, but their territory seems to have started near the present-day city of Stockton in the north, ranging south to just below the modern city of Madera. Northern Valley tribal land went east to the Sierra Nevada Mountain foothills and west to the top of the Diablo Mountain range. Over 31,000 people lived in this ideal part of California.

The Northern Valley tribes were not as fortunate as their Southern tribal neighbors when it came to water, however. Although the San Joaquin River ran through the center of their territory, there were no permanent streams of water throughout the year; except for the marshlands along the river where the tule canes grew, there was little plant life. Fortunately, grasses and flowering herbs grew in the spring-time and were collected, preserved, and stored by tribal women. Cottonwoods, willows, and groves of oak trees grew at the edges of the valley in this territory.

Climate in Northern Valley tribal land was much like that in the Southern Valley territory: very hot, dry summers and rainy winters. The only difference was that in the north, winters could become very cold, and rainfall often averaged up to 15 inches a year.

THE VILLAGE

Unlike most California tribes, Valley Yokuts spent most of the year at their permanent villages. They did not need many food-gathering campsites because the land around their villages supplied enough plant and animal life to feed them all year long.

Villages had two kinds of permanent homes. Most Northern Valley people lived in single family dwellings. These houses were just large enough for the one family, had an oval-shaped floor, wooden framework built by the men, and walls of large, woven tule mats made by the women.

Although Southern Yokuts built some smaller houses, like those of the northern tribelets, they usually built large homes, which housed as many as ten families. Valley Yokuts nearly always placed their houses in a straight line within the villages, possibly because most villages were built along river banks.

The larger houses also had a wood framework with poles brought together at the top. Steep roofs covered the long, many-family homes. Walls were of tule mats, which were also used inside the dwelling to section off a family from others living in the same house.

Each section had its own fireplace and door. Cooking and household work took place outside under a shade porch covered with tule mats. Inside were raised wood bed frames with tule mattresses laid on top of them. Bed frames were needed to keep mattresses off the damp floor in the lake areas of the Southern Yokuts territory. In drier areas, villagers dug the floor down into the ground a few feet. Tule mats were then placed on the dirt floors. Family belongings hung from the roof's framework or were stored in baskets leaning against the wall.

One of the most unusual things about the Southern Valley Yokuts was that their villages had no assembly building, or dance house. Nearly every other California tribe had large ceremonial buildings and/or dance enclosures, which were the sites of great feasts and ceremonies. Northern Valley Yokuts had at least one such huge dance lodge on the Little Panoche Creek in today's Fresno County. It is still there, and has been measured at 84 feet wide and 93 feet long.

In the Southern territory granaries were set up to store grain, dried fish, roots, seeds, and other foods. These storage buildings had mat-covered sides and were built up on legs to keep the food from becoming damp. If, by chance, a tree was nearby (trees would have been unusual there), food was then stored in storage baskets in its branches.

Each village had at least one sweathouse. This was usually a dirt-covered building, not over 15 feet long, where the village men did their daily sweating. Sweating was thought to be a way to cleanse and purify their bodies. Sometimes village men even slept in the sweathouse.

The more important, larger villages of the Northern Valley Yokuts were usually found either on top of low mounds of ground or near the banks of the San Joaquin River. Village sites were probably placed on higher ground to help keep houses and belongings dry during spring flooding season. Even with the yearly flooding, many of these tribelet village sites stayed in the same place for generations.

Tribelet land was owned by all tribelet members and food and water found on their land was available to everyone within their group. Some tribelets had only one village, others had several villages. Where there were several villages, the tribelet chief lived in the largest village.

VILLAGE LIFE

Southern Valley Yokuts had no one leader over their whole tribe. It had far too many people, so each tribelet governed itself with at least one chief. Historians have noted that the Yokuts were quite 'chief happy.' One tribelet had two chiefs for each village!

In both Valley Yokut tribes, the tribelet chiefs were very powerful. They set the dates for their annual mourning ceremony and other ceremonies; decided the winner between village contests; organized families to go on food-gathering and trading trips to other tribes; and were in charge of helping the poor and helpless of their tribelets.

A chief also got a portion of money from trade with other tribelets, and took a share of any payment received by village shamans (curing doctors) and dancers. A chief loaned money to his people at a high rate of interest, as well.

Even with all the money he got, he was often not the richest person in his villages; he had to take care of his poorer villagers, pay for all food and gifts at feasts, and in addition, he bought anything needed by his villages. Although he had great power over his own tribelet or village, a chief had little power anywhere else, other than being treated with great respect by neighbors.

A chief was helped by two assistants. One was called a messenger. One of a messenger's main duties was to carry invitation strings to other villages, officially notifying them of an upcoming ceremonial-feast. The number of knots on each invitation string showed how many days were left until a planned celebration. A messenger was also in charge of handing out food at large feasts and ceremonies.

The other important assistant to a chief was the speaker. A speaker had the duty of announcing any messages from the chief to villagers. This was an inherited job, like the chief's job. A speaker was paid by the chief to do work for him..

Usually the son of a chief followed his father in that job, but a younger brother or the brother's son could become chief. Once in a while the chief's daughter or sister was chosen, but this did not happen very often.

Families took animal names for themselves and their relatives. It was believed the animal name for their family was sacred, so no family member could eat meat from an animal for which their family was named.

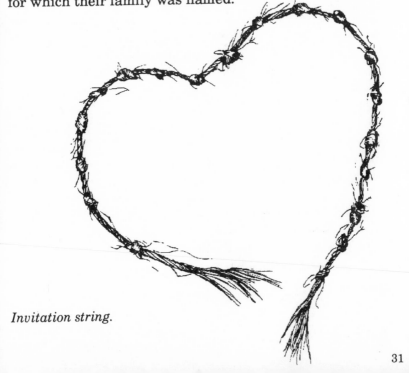

Invitation string.

Names like Magpie family, or Dove family, or Eagle family are examples of how families were told apart in a village. The most important family was called the Eagle family and usually meant the chief's family. When a new chief had to be chosen, he or she had to be from the Eagle family. Just as the chief came from the Eagle family, the messenger was known to be of the Dove family, and the speaker from the Magpie family.

Both Northern and Southern Valley Yokuts tribes were mostly peaceful. They did not go to war very often. In fact, the tribelets were quite friendly to other tribelets around them and unselfishly shared their food and water with those who needed them.

If war became necessary, usually tribelets joined together to fight an enemy. The Valley Yokuts did not even have a war chief, so if a war had to be fought, a brave villager volunteered to lead the way to battle.

Wars were announced to another tribe by way of a messenger, in most cases. Surprise attacks were not common. Usually, these wars were so small that only one or two warriors might be killed. Warriors especially tried to kill any shamans on the enemy's side. In the Yokut style of war there were no dances before or after a battle.

Newborn babies were most important to any village. Special diets were followed by those women about to have babies. The eating of meat was forbidden. Mostly, the diet was made up of good plant foods. Usually a mother-to-be ate roasted tule root.

Each baby was born in the family house. A new mother spent the first few weeks after the baby was born lying in a bed of warm stones, until she was well enough to begin taking care of the child herself.

Both of the new parents also followed strict tribal laws the first few months after a child was born. The new mother stayed on a special diet, did no cooking or basketmaking, and did not travel from her village. The new father had to stay indoors and could not hunt or go to the sweathouse for two months. The main reason for such rules was probably to make sure parents stayed close to a new baby, giving it every possible chance to grow into a strong adult.

A baby's first cradle was made of soft tule fiber. Later the baby was bound into a sturdier cradle attached to a Y-forked stick frame, where the child stayed until the age of walking. The stem end of the Y was stuck into the ground at a spot near to where the mother worked.

Babies were named about three or four weeks after birth. The family invited guests to the ceremony and fed those guests who brought gifts. Names chosen came from either side of the family, often being the name of some dead relative.

There were no teenager ceremonies for boys in the Valley Yokut tribes, but the teenage girls were usually tattooed and had a small, family feast at some time early in their teens, to celebrate their becoming adults.

When a young man became old enough to marry, his family took gifts of clothing or shell-bead money to the family of a suitable girl. This let the girl and her family know the young man's family was interested in there being a marriage between the two young people. If the girl's family approved, they gave the young man's family gifts of baskets and food. A feast was then held to celebrate the coming marriage. Sometimes these agreements were made while the boy and girl were still children. Then the marriage had to wait until they became old enough to be married.

For about a year after the marriage, a young couple lived with the bride's parents. Then the newlyweds moved to the young man's village to live out their life together. Tribal law did not allow the young man to speak directly to his mother-in-law, or the bride to speak to her father-in-law.

The wife gathered, prepared, and cooked all food. She also wove mats and baskets and made clothing. The bridegroom hunted and fished for his family, made and repaired fishing nets, and made hunting weapons and other tools needed for everyday life.

Older tribal members handled chores which took a great deal of time, since they had more time to spare. Often they looked after their grandchildren, training them how to perform the chores they would need to know as adults. Grandfathers taught young boys how to hunt and fish. Grandmothers taught the girls how to cook, sew, and gather food.

Children also had much free time to play. Their games were not too different from those of modern children.

When a tribal member died, a paid undertaker immediately prepared the body for burial. The dead body was tightly bound, placed into a grave in the village cemetery, with the head facing west, or northwest. West was the direction tribal members thought the land-of-the-dead was located. A village cemetery was always outside the village itself. Personal belongings of the dead persons were buried with them.

Those people who died away from home were cremated (burned). Some tribelets cremated all important villagers, whether or not they were at home. After these people were burned their bones, all that remained after the fire, were placed into a grave in the cemetery.

Only the wife, children, and parents of the dead person mourned in a ritualistic way. A widow cut her hair and did not wash her face for a period of time. She stayed in her house for as long as three months after the death, or at least until a mourning ceremony was celebrated. She also stayed on a strict diet to show her sorrow. Men relatives did no hunting until after a funeral, or mourning ceremony. The dead person's name was never again spoken aloud in front of relatives, unless it was given to a newborn child.

It was tribal belief that a dead person's soul left the grave two days after death and traveled west, or northwest, to the afterworld where there was a wide river spanned by a narrow bridge. The bridge was very hard to cross because it moved up and down. Dead persons had to cross that moving bridge before they could enter the afterworld.

Valley Yokuts believed the afterworld was a place where everyone slept by day and danced and enjoyed life during the night. They also felt that dead people lived in the land-of-the-dead surrounded by the same people they had lived with on earth, so they were never lonely.

RELIGION, MYTHS, AND BELIEFS

Most religious ceremonies had to do with funerals and mourning rituals. The number of these ceremonies depended on how many villagers had died during a year. Usually, ceremonies were full of dancing and singing and lasted about six days. Outsiders were invited, and a feast ended the celebration.

Often dancers would symbolize the dead people being honored. Visiting shamans used their spiritual powers to try to bring back a dead person. These shaman bring-them-back-to-life contests were exciting to everyone. Mourning ceremonies, as you can see, were not sad affairs; much laughter and game playing went on at such events.

Valley Yokut shamans, or spirit doctors, were the religious leaders of each village. Most of them were men. They claimed their power came from a vision or a dream. They believed that spirits lived in animals, or in monsters which lived in water.

As with shamans of other California tribes, Yokut shamans were most useful to their villagers as curing doctors. Shamans used sleight-of-hand tricks, like modern magicians, to diagnose a sickness so they could cure it. They pretended to suck a sickness from an ill person's body, magically pulling out some object which they claimed represented the sickness. That object could be anything from a small rock to a dead snake.

Shamans were paid great sums of money for their power. If a sick person began getting better during the curing dance, or the healing ritual, the shaman often asked for more money before completing the "cure."

A shaman shared his payments with the village chief. In return for sharing a shaman's payment, the chief would promise to protect the doctor from relatives of people he had failed to cure earlier. Even with this protection, many shamans still were killed by unhappy relatives. The job of being curing doctor was a risky one.

In many other tribes, a weather shaman was given great respect. The Valley Yokut groups did not need this kind of doctor, for their climate was good and did not need to be changed. However, these tribes had special shamans to whom they gave great respect, such as Bear shamans. Bear shamans were supposed to have the ability to change into bears. This belief sometimes helped keep angry relatives of a still sick, or dead person from getting too close to a Bear shaman who did not cure well. Villagers had great fear of Bear shamans.

Some curing methods used in early days would probably still work today. To keep from getting a cold, tribal members smeared red clay on their chests. A bad cough was treated by boiling horehound in water and then drinking it. Many herbal remedies used by modern doctors today, have come from the old tribal cures used by Native Americans.

Valley Yokuts believed that good and bad spirits lived in certain places. They felt that water babies with long black hair lived in ponds around them and were not friendly to humans. They also believed that a big snake with a human head lived underground. Tribal members feared these supposed spiritual animals, as well as others like them.

The religious ritual number for the Valley Yokuts was six. For example, religious rituals might have to last six days, or six people might always be needed to perform a ritual dance. Religious ceremonies took place in the open in Valley Yokut villages, since the Yokuts did not build dance houses.

An eclipse was explained to youngsters by saying a creature (maybe Coyote) was eating the sun or the moon. A dance was performed in some tribelets, using older women to pray for the creature to leave a part of the sun or moon for villagers.

Myths were not as important in the Valley Yokuts tribes as they were in neighboring tribes. Tribal members did have a creation myth, however. It was about Eagle, who had water birds dive for mud after the whole earth became flooded. None was able to bring up any mud until the littlest mud hen, dying from its great effort, finally brought up a tiny bit. According to the story, Eagle molded the tiny bit of mud and mixed it with some seeds, which swelled and became our land as we now know it.

Some designs found on the walls of cavelike places in the foothills of Southern Valley Yokuts territory are thought to be religious designs. Southern Valley Yokuts also said short prayers to spirits, made offerings of seed meal to spirit-gods, and sang sacred songs to honor their religion.

Nonreligious ceremonies were given in honor of food, in most cases to make sure the harvest was good each year. A First-Fruit ceremony was celebrated each year to honor berries. No berries could be eaten until the ceremony had been celebrated. Every ceremony ended with a feast.

FOOD

Since fish could be caught all year long, they were a main part of Southern Valley Yokut diet. Lake trout were the most prized and tasty fish to villagers. Other fish, such as perch or suckers, were also eaten. Steelhead salmon were caught during their trips upstream to lay eggs.

Northern Valley Yokuts also caught spawning salmon and large white sturgeons. Like the Southern Valley Yokuts, Northern Valley people did not often kill large animals for their meat. All Valley Yokuts seemed to like fish more than animal meat.

Fish was usually cooked by broiling it over hot coals. If many fish were caught, some were sun-dried and stored for winter food.

Although no records have been found on how they were caught, water birds, such as ducks, geese, and mudhens were eaten by the Northern Valley group. Probably snares or nets were used to capture them, or maybe they used the Southern Valley tribelets' method of catching them with long-handled nets as they took flight.

Many times the Southern Valley group hunted birds from fishing rafts. Hunters would cover themselves with tule and float close to the resting birds so they could shoot them with bows and arrows.

Another way the Southern Valley Yokuts caught water birds was to attach arrows to woven tule rings. Hunters threw the tule rings so they skipped across the surface of the water toward the birds, causing the arrow to hit a floating bird. This tribe also caught birds using stuffed-bird decoys. Birds' eggs were a favorite food of tribal members, too.

When hunters heard large flocks of geese coming, a huge pile of brush was set afire. The curious geese would fly low o see the fire, coming close enough for hunters to kill them with arrows.

Both Valley tribes depended a great deal on plant food for their meals. Acorns, along with fish, were certainly the main part of their daily diet. Acorn nuts were mashed, leached, and cooked into mush or bread. More about the preparing of acorns is found in Chapter One of this book.

Wild seeds and some roots were nearly as important as acorns. A flour made from pounded and dried tule roots was cooked into mush for a healthy meal. Many grass seeds and herbs were processed in the same way as the roots. Grassnut roots were usually roasted whole for eating. Salt to season foods came from the salt-grass plant.

Twined basketry hopper in place on mortar stone.

Food which had to be boiled was placed in a watertight basket. Water and steaming hot rocks from the fire were added to the food. The hot rocks were tossed about the basket with a looped branch from a tree until the food was cooked. Tossing the rocks kept them from burning the baskets while food was cooking. Another way of cooking food was to bake it in small beehive-shaped earth ovens.

In some of the more desert-like areas of the valley, oak trees were few and far between. Tribelets living in those places traded with eastern tribes, whose territories had groves of oak trees. Valley Yokut tribelets offered fish in trade for the acorns they needed.

Wood for fires had to come from trees, and any kind of tree was hard to find in drier parts of the San Joaquin Valley. In order to save what wood tribal members could find, tule was dried and burned with it to make cooking and heating fires last longer.

Few insects were eaten by either tribe, and although skunks were eaten, frogs, eagles, and hawks were never eaten.

HUNTING AND FISHING

Fishermen had many ways to catch fish. One method was to tie one end of a long net to a pole on shore. The other end of the net was held by a villager who was seated on a raft. The raft moved in a half circle, coming back to shore, causing the net to become circular. It was then dragged ashore by tribesmen. Large numbers of fish were trapped in this manner.

Wide, flat tule rafts, with a spear hole in the center of each, were sometimes used in very shallow water. Fish passing beneath the raft could be speared through the hole. At other times the men dove for fish using hand nets to catch them.

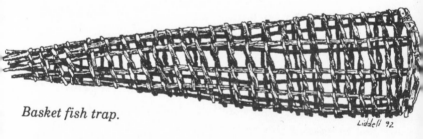

Basket fish trap.

Basket traps were another way to catch fish. Most basket traps were shaped like a cone. A fish could easily swim forward into the trap but could not swim backwards out of it.

Like most other California tribal fishermen, the Valley Yokuts sometimes dropped part of the turkey mullein plant into quiet places of rivers or streams. This plant poisoned

40

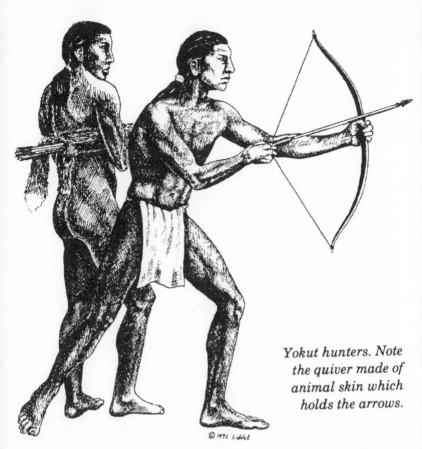

Yokut hunters. Note the quiver made of animal skin which holds the arrows.

© 1992 Liddell

fish just enough to paralyze them, causing them to float to the top of the water so they could be picked up by waiting fishermen. Fortunately, this type of poison did not harm humans.

Mass hunts were held by tribal hunters in desert areas of the valley to catch jackrabbits. Ground squirrels were smoked, flooded, or prodded out of their ground homes. Larger animals, although not hunted as much, were killed with bows and arrows shot by men hiding in tall tule reeds or were caught by traps set with loops of cord. This kind of trap caught deer and elk by their antlers, the cord tightly holding animals until hunters could kill them.

Weapons used to shoot large animals were like those used to fight a war. The bow was backed with sinew (stretchy animal tendons) to make them bend easily without breaking. Arrows for this kind of hunting or fighting had sharp stone arrowheads attached to them. Smaller animals were killed with an all-wooden arrow. Small boys learned to shoot a bow with this one-piece all-wood arrow.

TOOLS AND UTENSILS

Baskets were used in every part of tribal life. Bowl-shaped baskets made excellent cooking containers. The cone-shaped burden baskets women carried on their backs carried everything from acorns to belongings, as the tribal members moved from permanent villages to food-gathering sites. If a heavy load was carried on a woman's head, a round ring of tule fiber was placed underneath the load to make it more stable, less apt to tip over. The ring also acted as a cushion, protecting the woman's head from the load's weight.

Flat winnowing trays helped women separate husks from grass seeds and grains they were getting ready to grind into flour. As the grain was thrown up into the wind, the lighter husk would blow away, and the heavier grain or seed would fall back into the tray.

Most everyday baskets were made with the twined method of weaving. Seed beaters, water bottles sealed with tar, and storage baskets all were twined by the women. The Southern Valley Yokuts had one unusual basket not found in other tribes. It was a sifting basket made of tule fiber and bound with string.

The more artistic baskets were made using the coiling method. These baskets usually had decorations woven into them. Redbud branches had a reddish color which could be woven into the basket in the form of a design. Bright feathers were often used to decorate these baskets, which were woven more for show than for usefulness.

Wood was used for fire-making drills, mush stirrers, the smaller mortars and pestles, bows and arrows, and digging sticks used to harvest roots.

Stone made fine tools. Knives were made from stone, as were arrow points and scraping tools used in processing animal hides. Yokuts traded with other tribes to get stone mortars and pestles. Awls, which were used to make holes in skins, were made from sharp, pointed animal bones.

Canoes and rafts needed for fishing, or for traveling from one place to another, were made from the important tule plants. Canoes were made of dried bundles of tule cane, tightly tied. The canoe, called a balsa boat, was narrow across, had a bow which was higher than the back of the boat, and was steered with rounded paddles.

TRADE

As with every California tribe, Valley Yokuts traded with other tribes to get items they could not find in their territory. From the Salinan tribe Yokuts got shell beads for money strings. From the Chumash tribes they got steatite (soapstone) bowls which had originally come from the Gabrielinos. From the Costanoans (Ohlone) tribes, Northern Valley Yokuts traded for mussels, abalone shells and other seashore products.

Southern Valley Yokuts traded fish, salt from salt-grass, seed foods, and many kinds of herbs to the Chumash tribe for all kinds of shells. Many of the whole shells they got from the Chumash were then traded to the Salinan tribe.

Those items a tribe needed, and for which they had no products of equal value to offer in trade, were bought with shell-bead money. Shell beads were made from broken bits of clamshells and strung on fiber strings of an exact length. To tribal members, these strings were like our money today. The most valuable money strings were those which had perfectly matched beads, both in color and in shape.

CLOTHING

Dancing costumes were very fancy and colorful. One such costume was made up of a short skirt of eagle down feathers which had been twisted between milkweed fiber strings. At the bottom ends of the strings, hawk feathers had been tied. A headdress of magpie tail feathers was worn with the skirt. Often dancers' faces were painted in patterns symbolizing the animal name of their particular family.

Everyday clothing was not nearly as bright as dancing costumes. Valley Yokut men wore only a deerskin breechclout, or nothing. Children wore no clothes except in cold weather. Women always wore a double apron with the narrow front piece fringed at the bottom, and the back piece made larger than the front. Apron fabric was usually shredded tule canes, woven marsh grass, mudhen skins, or rabbitskins.

In very cold weather, both men and women wrapped themselves in cloaks, or capes, made of woven mudhen or rabbitskins. The cloak was used as a blanket on cool nights.

Yokut shaman's hat; worn during ritual events.

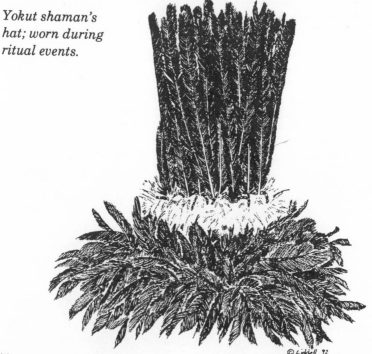

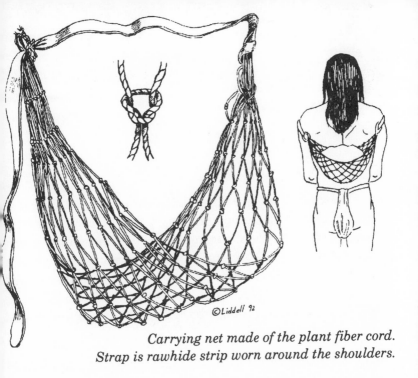

Carrying net made of the plant fiber cord.
Strap is rawhide strip worn around the shoulders.

Most tribal members went barefoot, except when traveling. For journeys, moccasins of deer or elk skins were worn in rocky, brush-filled country. Men carried their belongings for a trip in carrying nets they made out of fishing net cord.

They wore no head coverings. Women wore basket caps when they were carrying a heavy burden basket on their backs. A burden basket had netting which was placed around the women's foreheads to give their backs better support when they carried heavy loads. The basket hats helped to keep pressure from the netting off the women's foreheads.

Both men and women wore their hair long and free, except when they worked. Then it was gathered up in a string at the back of the neck. Valley Yokuts did not do much tattooing. When girls became teenagers, their chins were tattooed with their family symbols. Men seldom wore any tattoos.

Small children had their ears pierced, and sometimes the nose bone was also pierced. Wood, bone, or shell ornaments were worn in the holes. One shell that was very valuable to the Valley Yokuts was the long, slender clamshell hinge of a rock clamshell. So precious was this hinge that it was used in the center of bead necklaces. This bit of shell was even more valuable than money.

MUSIC AND GAMES

Songs of the Valley Yokuts mostly were sung in religious rituals, much as church choirs sing hymns today. Words to the songs were few and were not easy to understand. Split-stick rattles might beat the rhythm for songs but cocoon rattles, bone and wood whistles, and flutes, were also played as accompaniment. The only California Native American stringed instrument, a nose harp, was played by members of Valley Yokuts tribelets.

There was one hand game which used singing. Called Wikchammi, the game used a group of women who sang in answer to the singing of a group of men. Another pleasure using music was dancing, which was performed during most big festival events and at religious ceremonies.

Adults loved to play games of chance in their spare time. In one hand game, dice made from walnut halfshells were used. The walnuts were filled with a tar, and bits of abalone shells were added as decorations.

Dice made by women for their games of chance. Walnut halves are filled with tar with bits of shells added as decoration.

© Liddell 92

Teams of men played each other in many field games. Shinny (which used a stick much like a modern hockey stick), ball games, and stick races like relays were all played.

In one game, called hoop-and-pole, players aimed poles at rolling stone hoops to see if the pole could be thrown through the moving targets. Another favorite game the men played was trying to throw a ball, or shoot an arrow through a ring fastened to the top of a tall pole. Maybe this could have been an ancient kind of basketball.

HISTORY

The Valley Yokuts tribe was known to have first met white men just three years after the first Spanish mission was built in California territory. Spanish soldiers visited a village on the edge of Buena Vista Lake in 1772. However, from that time until 1802, the tribes mostly were left alone. As the 1800s began, a Spanish California governor joined with some of the mission churches in an effort to build more missions, especially in the San Joaquin Valley. This was not a successful plan. Very few of the lake tribelet people became mission Indians.

Some runaway mission Indians did come to live with the Valley Yokuts during this time, however. Much of the new information they had learned and seen at the missions was discussed with Yokuts tribal men. The lake-area Yokuts especially liked what they heard about horses found at the missions.

California Native Americans had never seen horses until European explorers brought them to the California territory. Horses could be very useful to tribal members, who had always walked or floated on water to travel.

The Valley Yokuts and their mission Indian friends began to raid mission ranchos, taking horses. So clever did they become that they actually earned the name of "horse thief Indians."

In 1833, Mexicans infected with a disease called malaria came too close to the lake-area Yokuts. Seventy-five percent of the tribal members died from the disease. Mexicans were followed by white American settlers who began to settle on tribal land. The Valley Yokuts fought hard for their land but were too few and too weak from the malaria to protect their property.

The United States government at first made a deal with the tribes, offering them reservation land and money in return for tribal land. The government never got senate approval for this treaty. Instead, tribal members were simply taken to a reservation. Settlers continued to settle on Yokut land, ignoring sacred areas such as cemeteries and plowing up fields of tribal seed food.

In 1970, about 325 Southern Valley Yokuts were still living on the Tule River reservation. At that time, they had a rather stable economy. Some men worked in the lumber industry making money selling their own timber. Many tribal members worked in orchards picking fruit certain times of the year.

Although they are not as poor as some other tribespeople today, not enough of the young Yokut people are graduating from high school and college. Only bits of the old Yokut tribal life still continue. Each year, as more of the older tribal members die, more memories of old tribal life are lost. Let us hope that soon the Valley Yokuts will join other Native Americans in our land as they begin to reclaim their heritage.

NORTHERN AND SOUTHERN VALLEY YOKUTS

OUTLINE

GLOSSARY

AWL: a sharp, pointed tool used for making small holes in leather or wood

CEREMONY: a meeting of people to perform formal rituals for a special reason; like an awards ceremony to hand out trophies to those who earned honors

CHERT: rock which can be chipped off, or flaked, into pieces with sharp edges

COILED: a way of weaving baskets which looks like the basket is made of rope coils woven together

DIAMETER: the length of a straight line through the center of a circle

DOWN: soft, fluffy feathers

DROUGHT: a long period of time without water

DWELLING: a building where people live

FLETCHING: attaching feathers to the back end of an arrow to make the arrow travel in a straight line

GILL NET: a flat net hanging vertically in water to catch fish by their heads and gills

GRANARIES: basket-type storehouses for grains and nuts

HERITAGE: something passed down to people from their long-ago relatives

LEACHING: washing away a bitter taste by pouring water through foods like acorn meal

MORTAR: flat surface of wood or stone used for the grinding of grains or herbs with a pestle

PARCHING: to toast or shrivel with dry heat

PESTLE: a small stone club used to mash, pound, or grind in a mortar

PINOLE: flour made from ground corn

INDIAN RESERVATION: land set aside for Native Americans by the United States government

RITUAL: a ceremony that is always performed the same way

SEINE NET: a net which hangs vertically in the water, encircling and trapping fish when it is pulled together

SHAMAN: tribal religious men or women who use magic to cure illness and speak to spirit-gods

SINEW: stretchy animal tendons

STEATITE: a soft stone (soapstone) mined on Catalina Island by the Gabrielino tribe; used for cooking pots and bowls

TABOO: something a person is forbidden to do

TERRITORY: land owned by someone or by a group of people

TRADITION: the handing down of customs, rituals, and belief, by word of mouth or example, from generation to generation

TREE PITCH: a sticky substance found on evergreen tree bark

TWINING: a method of weaving baskets by twisting fibers, rather than coiling them around a support fiber

NATIVE AMERICAN WORDS
WE KNOW AND USE

PLANTS AND TREES
hickory
pecan
yucca
mesquite
saguaro

ANIMALS
caribou
chipmunk
cougar
jaguar
opossum
moose

STATES
Dakota – friend
Ohio – good river
Minnesota – waters that
  reflect the sky
Oregon – beautiful water
Nebraska – flat water
Arizona
Texas

FOODS
avocado
hominy
maize (corn)
persimmon
tapioca
succotash

GEOGRAPHY
bayou – marshy body of
  water
savannah – grassy plain
pasadena – valley

WEATHER
blizzard
Chinook (warm, dry wind)

FURNITURE
hammock

HOUSE
wigwam
wickiup
tepee
igloo

INVENTIONS
toboggan

BOATS
canoe
kayak

OTHER WORDS
caucus – group meeting
mugwump – loner politician
squaw – woman
papoose – baby

CLOTHING
moccasin
parka
mukluk – slipper
poncho

BIBLIOGRAPHY

Cressman, L. S. *Prehistory of the Far West.* Salt Lake City, Utah: University of Utah Press, 1977.

Geiger, Maynard, O.F.M., Ph.D. *The Indians of Mission Santa Barbara.* Santa Barbara, CA 93105: Franciscan Fathers, 1986.

Heizer, Robert F., volume editor. *Handbook of North American Indians; California, volume 8.* Washington, D.C.: Smithsonian Institute, 1978.

Heizer, Robert F. and Elsasser, Albert B. *The Natural World of the California Indians.* Berkeley and Los Angeles, CA; London, England: University of California Press, 1980.

Heizer, Robert F. and Whipple, M.A.. *The California Indians.* Berkeley and Los Angeles, CA; London, England: University of California Press, 1971.

Heuser, Iva. *California Indians.* PO Box 352, Camino, CA 95709: Sierra Media Systems, 1977.

Macfarlen, Allen and Paulette. *Handbook of American Indian Games.* 31 E. 2nd Street, Mineola, N.Y. 11501: Dover Publications, 1985.

Murphey, Edith Van Allen. *Indian Uses of Native Plants.* 603 W. Perkins Street, Ukiah, CA 95482: Mendocino County Historical Society, © renewal, 1987.

National Geographic Society. *The World of American Indians.* Washington, DC: National Geographic Society reprint, 1989.

Tunis, Edwin. *Indians.* 2231 West 110th Street, Cleveland, OH: The World Publishing Company, 1959.

Credits:
The Pollard Group, Inc., Tacoma, Washington 98409
Dona McAdam, Mac on the Hill, Seattle, Washington 98109

Acknowledgements:
Kim Walters, Library Director, and Richard Buchen,
Research Librarian, Braun Library, Southwest Museum
Special thanks

4799